221655

This **Picture Mammoth** *belongs to*

_____

_____

LONG AGO

dinosaurs   diplodocus   stegosaurus   rocket

crocodiles   gangplank   buffaloes   pelicans porcupines dove antelope

NOAH'S ARK

volcano sparks lava

ferocious tyrannosaurus rex

FAR AWAY

flying saucer

astronaut

spring

yramids

Earth

planets

woolly mammoth

igloo

cowboy jeans

cave cavepeople club bone

prickly pear cactus

for Mr Hardman, my first English teacher

alpha bravo charlie delta echo foxtrot golf hotel india juliet kilo lim

Jan Pieńkowski
1001 WORDS

...ke
oscar
november
papa
quebec
romeo
sierra
tango
uniform
victor
whiskey
x-ray
yankee
zulu

Picture mammoth

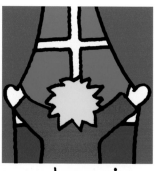

good morning

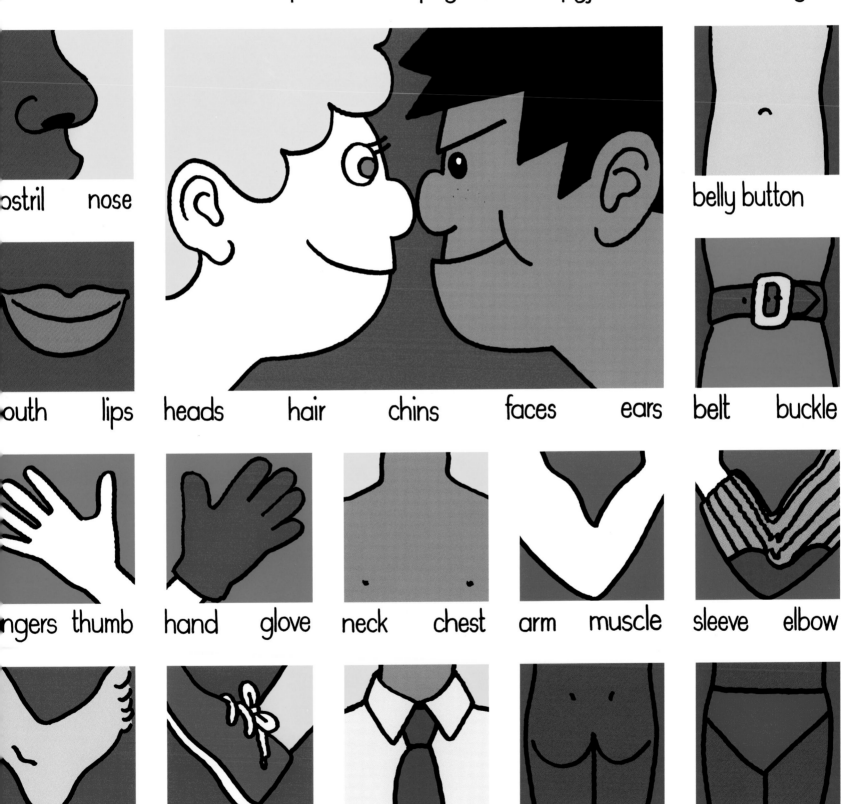

andkerchief trousers socks pants vest pegs t-shirt pyjamas clothes line tights

ostril nose

belly button

outh lips heads hair chins faces ears belt buckle

ngers thumb hand glove neck chest arm muscle sleeve elbow

nkle foot shoe lace collar tie bottom briefs

FOOD

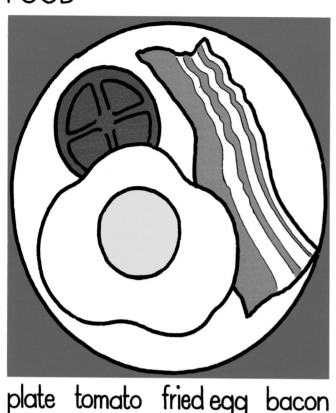

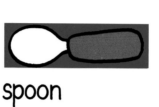
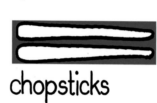

plate   tomato   fried egg   bacon

knife

fork

spoon

chopsticks

salad   lettuce   chees

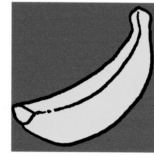

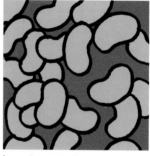

bread crumbs   banana   apple   bite   baked beans   biscuit

teapot   tablecloth   cereal   jug   kiwi fruit   pineapple   grapes   melo

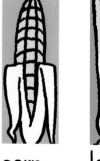

glass of milk   orange   plum   burger   bun   corn   leek

chicken   chips   ketchup   peas   sugar cubes   salt   pepper   cherry   chocolate cake   jam

avocado   butter dish   strawberry   hot dog   honey   jar

cook   pastry   pie   eat   lemon   slice   bib   messy   spill   drink   straw

onion   radish   rice   bowl   spaghetti   fishfinger   toaster   toast

FAMILY

grandma

grandpa

great grandma

grandfather

grandmother

aunt

girl   man   woman   boy

DAD MUM

daughter   father   mother   son

uncle

Prince

Sooty

older brother   younger sister

baby

cousins   twins

ogs   bitch   puppies   rabbits

ick insects   canaries   gerbil   scales   paws   tongue   sheepdog

uinea pigs   hutch   dandelions   hamster   tabby cat   whiskers   flap   eyes

kitten   boot   rat   tail   ants

air of budgies   perch   tropical fish   aquarium   bubbles   goldfish

HOME

 vacuum cleaner

 washing machine

 table

 chair

 cooker   po

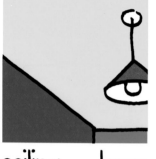 ceiling   lamp

 wall   corner

 floor   boards

pillow   sheet   blanket   radio   mug   cupboard

vase   window   curtains   sofa   mirror   clock

 door   kno

 doormat

 iron

 key

 telephone

 television

fridge

irdfeeder

lily

wasp

caterpillar

birdbath

over   leaf

fern   snail

hose   drop

uttercup

lawnmower

wheelbarrow   pumpkin   carrots

watering can

adybird

mole

rake

hoe

shears

is   bud

daisy

daffodil

tulip

rose

FUN

party hats   friends

tiptoe   hide and seek   he

walk   mud   puddle

skipping rope

piggyback

robot

hammer   nails

spanner

saw

playground   low   swing   high

ping pong

tic-tac-toe

frisbee

se   trip   hop   jump   sack race   win

irthday cake   laugh   romp

liers   screwdriver

ut and bolt   screw

dancer   tutu

light   seesaw   heavy

oomerang   jigsaw puzzle   yoyo   skeleton   trick or treat   witch

SCHOOL

clock

twelve hours   sixty minutes

zero   one   two   three   four   fiv

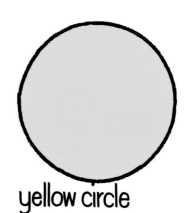

orange zigzag

yellow circle

green square

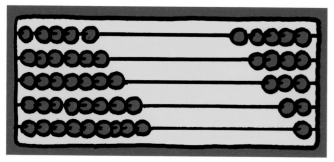

abacus   sums   wires   beads

black spiral

brown oval

red crescent

screen   keyboard   computer

trumpet

drum

paper   scissor

left   fists   right   half   quarte

6 six **7** seven **8** eight **9** nine **10** ten

urple triangle   tan rectangle   blue wave

easel   paint   picture   artist

hite star   grey diamond   pink heart

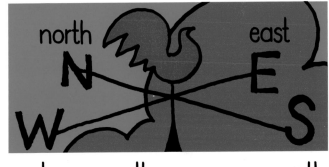

west   weather vane   south

aintbrush pen   pencil crayon   chalk   marker

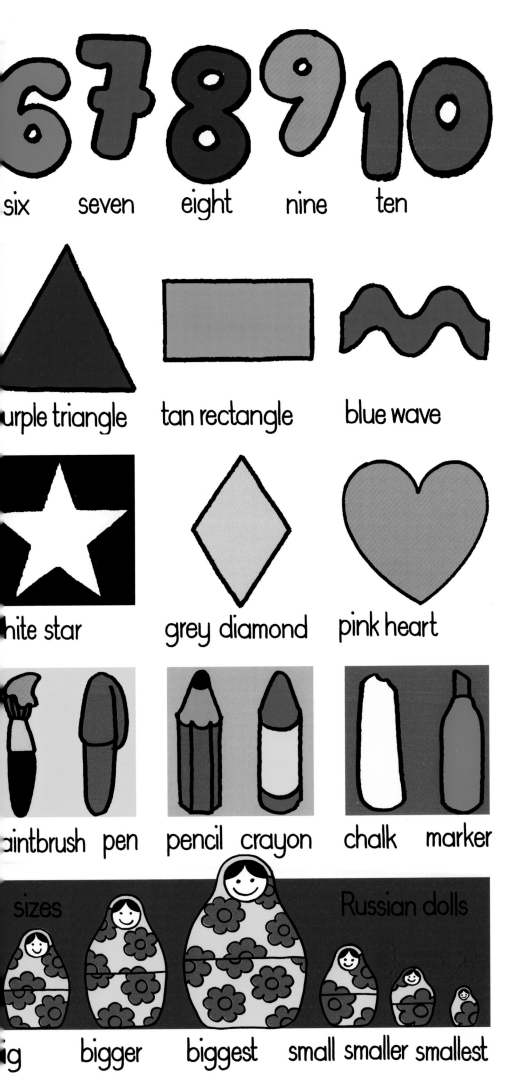

sizes   Russian dolls

ig   bigger   biggest   small smaller smallest

colours   shapes   building bricks

TOWN

RESTAURANT · street

COLOSS

chef · queue · lamppost · monster · poster · teacher · theatre · steps · drill · workmo

city

lift

fountain

carwash

magazine

mosque · crane · block of flats

up · escalator · dow

VEGETABLES

elery   tangerines   grapefruit   pears   cabbages

basket   crowd   people   feet

BAKER

oaves   rolls

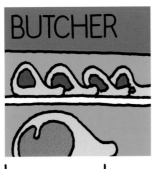

BUTCHER

ham   chops

pizza

lollipop   flowers

honey   carrier bag   juice   carton

AUGUST

monday   1
tuesday   2
wednesday   3
thursday   4
friday   5
saturday   6
sunday   7

calendar   week

GARAGE

petrol station   flat tyre   pump

TRAVEL

orchard   electric train   carriages   track   viaduct   valley   ruins   smoke   tunnel

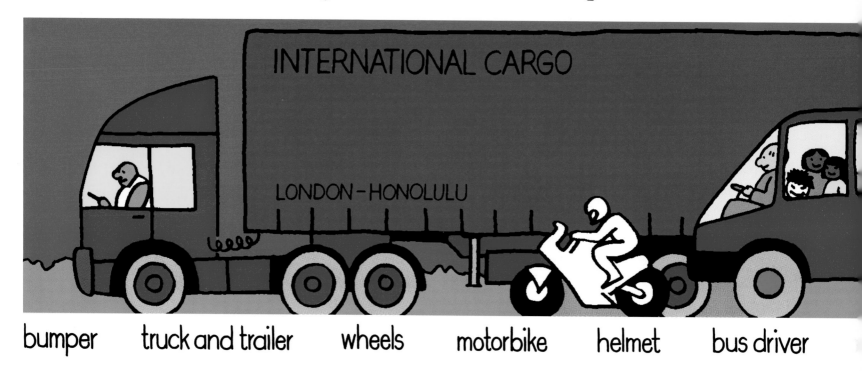

bumper   truck and trailer   wheels   motorbike   helmet   bus driver

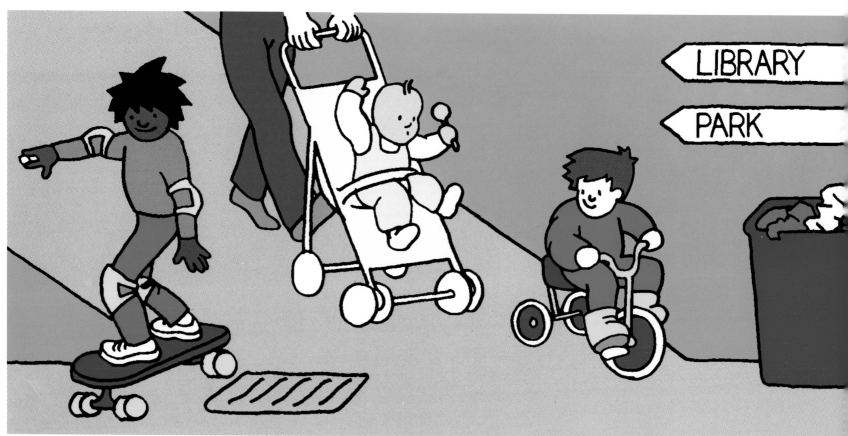

bandage   skateboard   drain   baby buggy   rattle   path   tricycle   grass   rubbish

caravan   tents   steam engine   church   houses   village   mountain   road

ers   breakdown truck   tipper   car   accident   digger   hubcap

post   blackbirds   roller skates   brake   wheelchair   bicycle   pedal   handlebar   rubble

HOLIDAYS

barbecue

pool   hammock   swim   float   postcards stamp

snowboard   skis   ski stick

canoe   paddles

umbrella

cap   sunglasses   candy floss

suitcase   labels

picnic   sandwich box   hamper   camera   strap   fairground   merry-go-round   ride

  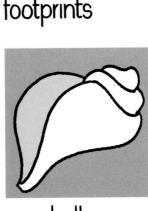 

footprints

urfer　　surfboard　　wave　　seashell　　kids　ball　shrimp net　sand

ab　claws　deckchair　　starfish　　goggles snorkel diver flippers

ice cream cone

ailing boat　sails　sailors　　bucket　spade　　beach　suntan　sandcastle　flag

SEA

octopus   storm   lightning

penguin   ice

eels   seaweed   se

lobster

walrus

dolphins

seagull

cliff   lighthouse   yacht   line

anchor   cable   fog

shark   fin   jaws

seahorse

whale   spout   ocea

rainbow

eagle

sun

rain　splash　raindrops

glider

swallow　fly

jet aeroplane　clouds

wind　scarf　kite　string

parachute

island　sunset　pilot　helicopter

FARM

tractor   farmer

cock

fox

farmya

hen   chicks

sheep

turkey

egg   goose

lamb

bull   horns

cow   c

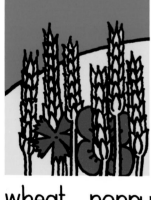  

wheat poppy

baby donkey

goat   udder

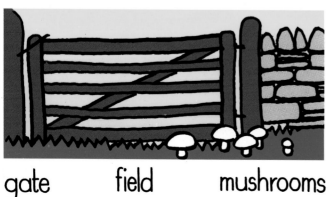  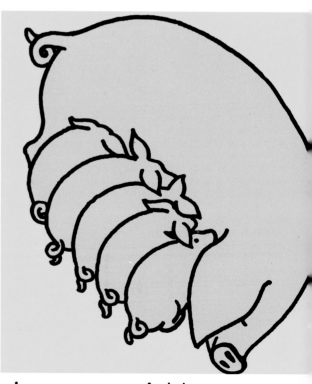

gate   field   mushrooms

bee

pigs   piglets   so

est   toad   mouse   hole   ducklings   ducks   pond

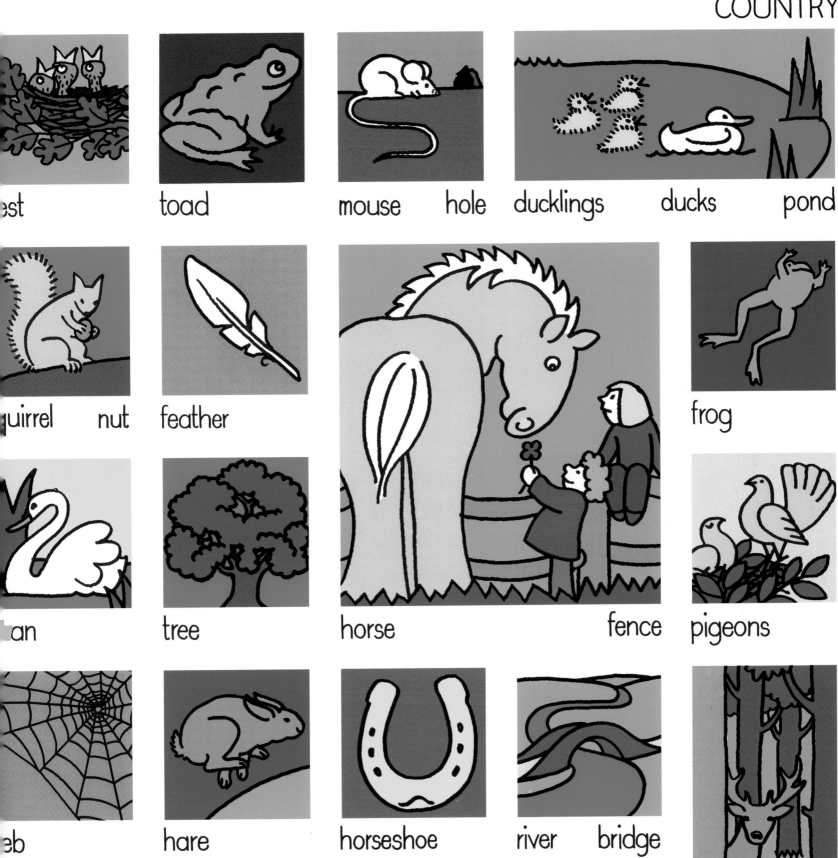

quirrel   nut   feather   frog

an   tree   horse   fence   pigeons

eb   hare   horseshoe   river   bridge

ony   saddle   rider   tadpole   windmill   deer   wood

WILD ANIMALS

gorilla

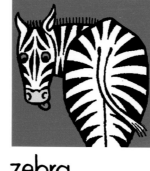

zebra

hippopotamus

kangaroo

koala

giraffe

camel   hump

panda

peacock

flamingo

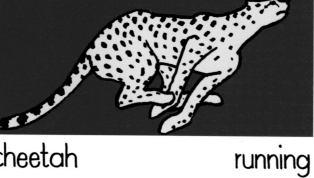

cheetah   running

elephant   trunk

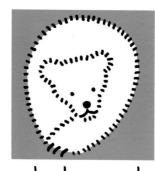

polar bear cub

lion   man

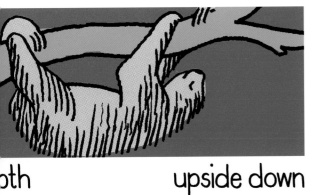  

oth upside down snake rhinoceros

urtle butterfly armadillo

hameleon vampire bat jaguar jungle tiger stripes

spider fangs toucan beak alligators

 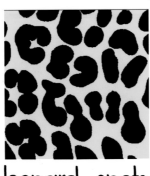 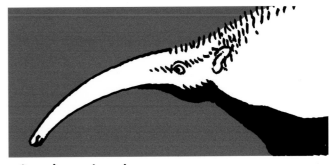

onkey parrot leopard spots giant anteater

STOP : GO

fast   slow   birds   tortoise crawling uphill   before   blow

go out   clean   come in   dirty   climb   branch

shout   loud   quiet   secret   whisper   alive   wet   flowerpo

balloon   after   push   stubborn   donkey   bareback   reins   pull

bump   fall   make   tube of glue   model   break

plant   dry   dead   hit   target   bull's-eye   arrows   miss

GETTING BETTER

trolley

nurse   chart   cape   hospital   furry toy   broken leg

love   hug   frien

ambulance

dentist   tooth

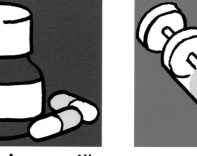

medicine   pills

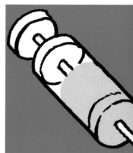

syring

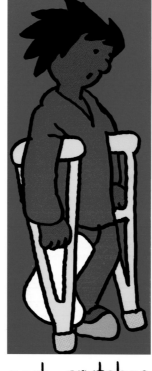

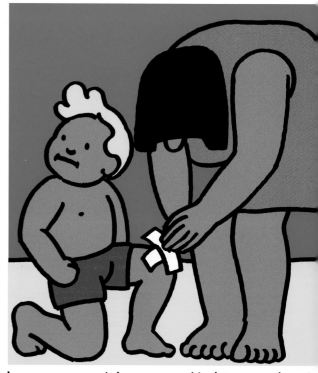

doctor   ill   thermometer   cot   cast   crutches

brave   cut knee   sticking plast

ate   fight   teddy bear   give   kind   gift   pleased   take

heeky   scared   happy   smile   tired   yawn   shy   blush

roud   stack of blocks   sad   tear   jealous   noise

angry   frown

CHRISTMAS

chimney   sleigh   Santa Claus   beard   roof top

pile of presents   parcel   ribbon

envelope   card   stocking

choir   carol singers

nativity play   kings   holy family   stable   shepherd

ndeer bells antlers hooves candle wax sledge speed downhill slope

holly berries

ow snowman pipe twigs snowflakes frost icicles branch robins

BEDTIME

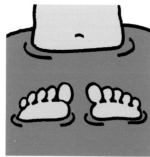

bath   toes

stairs   dressing gown slippers   soap   flannel   prayers nightlight patchwork qu

toothpaste   toothbrush   moon   night   comb   brush

shampoo

towel taps washbasin lavatory   cup of cocoa   storybook   page   duvet be

goodnight

DREAMS

angel harp

bride bridegroom

unicorn

castle   towers   battlements

barn owl

ruby ring

ghost

picture queen sceptre orb

knight armour shield spear charge

jewel

emerald sapp

galleon pirate ship   skull and crossbones

mermaid

fishtail

flames

firebreathing scaly dragon with spiky tail

pretty princess

padlock chain treasure pearls coins gold silver

First published in Great Britain 1994
by William Heinemann Ltd
Published 1998 by Mammoth
an imprint of Reed International Books Limited
Michelin House, 81 Fulham Road, London SW3 6RB

10 8 6 4 2 1 3 5 7 9

Copyright © Jan Pieńkowski 1994
Jan Pieńkowski has asserted his moral rights

ISBN 0 7497 2840 X

A CIP catalogue record for this title
is available from the British Library

Assembled and originated on computer by Jane Walmsley.
Lettering by Caroline Austin. Bitmap tracing by Jenny Thomas.
Computer technical adviser Brian Voakes.

Printed in Hong Kong by Wing King Tong Co. Ltd.